Biomass
Fueling Change

Niki Walker

Crabtree Publishing Company

www.crabtreebooks.com

Crabtree Publishing Company
www.crabtreebooks.com

Coordinating editor: Ellen Rodger

Series editor: Carrie Gleason

Project editor: Adrianna Morganelli

Editors: Rachel Eagen, L. Michelle Nielsen

Book design and production coordinator: Rosie Gowsell

Production assistant: Samara Parent

Art Director: Rob MacGregor

Photo research: Allison Napier

Photographs: Peter Bowater/Alamy: p. 13; Tomas Kopecny/Alamy: p. 11 (top); Maurice Joseph/Alamy: p. 1; AP/Wide World Photos: p. 14, p. 16, p. 17 (bottom), p. 20, p. 21 (bottom); Dane Andrew/ZUMA/Corbis: p. 28; Eleanor Bentall/Corbis: cover; Niall Benvie/Corbis: p. 27; Bettmann/Corbis: p. 23; Jonathan Blair/Corbis: p. 22; Corbis: p. 3 (bottom left); Nick Hawkes; Ecoscene/Corbis: p. 4; Zainal Abd Halim/Reuters/Corbis: p. 19 (top); Richard Hamilton Smith/Corbis: p. 26; Mike Kepka/San Francisco Chronicle/Corbis: p. 30 (bottom); Vince Streano/Corbis: p 10; Paulo Whitaker/Reuters/Corbis: p. 25; Betsy Dupuis/istock International: Rosie the riveter icon; Vanessa Vick/Photo Researchers, Inc.: p. 18; Reuters/David Mdzinarishvili: p. 15 (top); Reuters/Alex de la Rosa: p. 29; Reuters/Jayanta Shaw: p. 17 (top), p. 31 (bottom); other images from stock CD.

Illustrations: Margaret Amy Salter: p. 8

Cover: British Touring Car Championship driver Fiona Leggate's car runs on ethanol. Ethanol is a biofuel that is made from crops such as sugar cane, wheat, and corn.

Title page: Biomass has been used for energy since prehistoric times when people used wood to light fires for heat and light. This woman from Myanmar carries firewood that will be used for energy.

Library and Archives Canada Cataloguing in Publication

Walker, Niki, 1972-
    Biomass : fueling change / Niki Walker.

(Energy revolution)
Includes index.
ISBN-13: 978-0-7787-2914-3 (bound)
ISBN-10: 0-7787-2914-1 (bound)
ISBN-13: 978-0-7787-2928-0 (pbk.)
ISBN-10: 0-7787-2928-1 (pbk.)

    1. Biomass energy--Juvenile literature. I. Title. II. Series.

TP339.W34 2006   j333.95'39   C2006-902856-7

Library of Congress Cataloging-in-Publication Data

Biomass : fueling change / written by Niki Walker.
    p. cm.
    Includes index.
    ISBN-13: 978-0-7787-2914-3 (rlb)
    ISBN-10: 0-7787-2914-1 (rlb)
    ISBN-13: 978-0-7787-2928-0 (pbk)
    ISBN-10: 0-7787-2928-1 (pbk)
    1. Biomass energy--Juvenile literature. I. Title.

TP339.W35 2006
333.95'39--dc22
                              2006016035

Crabtree Publishing Company

www.crabtreebooks.com   1-800-387-7650

Copyright © **2007 CRABTREE PUBLISHING COMPANY**. All rights reserved. No part of this publication may be reproduced, stored in a retrieval system or be transmitted in any form or by any means, electronic, mechanical, photocopying, recording, or otherwise, without the prior written permission of Crabtree Publishing Company. In Canada: We acknowledge the financial support of the Government of Canada through the Book Publishing Industry Development Program (BPIDP) for our publishing activities.

Published in Canada
Crabtree Publishing
616 Welland Ave.
St. Catharines, ON
L2M 5V6

Published in the United States
Crabtree Publishing
PMB16A
350 Fifth Ave., Suite 3308
New York, NY 10118

Published in the United Kingdom
Crabtree Publishing
White Cross Mills
High Town, Lancaster
LA1 4XS

Published in Australia
Crabtree Publishing
386 Mt. Alexander Rd.
Ascot Vale (Melbourne)
VIC 3032

Contents

Energy Conservation: 'We Can Do It!'

"We Can Do It" was a slogan that appeared on posters made during World War II. One poster featured "Rosie the Riveter," a woman dressed in blue coveralls (shown below). The poster was originally intended to encourage women to enter into the workforce to fill non-traditional roles as workers in industry. Today, the image of Rosie the Riveter has come to represent a time when people came together as a society to reach a common goal. Today's energy challenge can be combatted in a similar way. Together, we can work to save our planet from the pollution caused by burning fossil fuels, by learning to conserve energy and develop alternative energy sources.

We Can Do It!

WAR PRODUCTION CO-ORDINATING COMMITTEE

Energy in Our Lives

Energy is the capacity to do work or make something happen. Without energy, there would be no life on Earth. Energy is used to cook food, heat buildings, and make humans, animals, and plants live and grow. Every machine on the planet, including cars, televisions, computers, and the factories that make them, run on energy.

In the United States, biomass is the most commonly used renewable energy source. Recycling bins are reserved specifically for biomass, such as this bin for garden waste.

What is Biomass?

Biomass is the name for all **organisms** on Earth and their wastes. Biomass that is used for energy includes grasses, trees, and other plants. Sawdust, woodchips, food scraps, animal dung, and sewage are also used for biomass. Biomass stores solar energy, or energy from the Sun, and converts it into **chemical energy**. When biomass is burned, eaten and **digested**, or turned into gases or liquid fuels, its energy is released. The energy we receive from biomass is called bioenergy. It is used for heating, cooking, lighting, running cars and trucks, and producing electricity.

Green garden waste only

No plastic bags

Energy Sources

Anything that has energy people can use is an energy source. There are two basic types of energy sources: non-renewable and renewable sources. Non-renewable sources cannot be replaced once they are used, and will run out someday. Fossil fuels, such as coal, oil, and natural gas, are non-renewable. Renewable sources, which are also called alternative energy sources, are continually replaced by people or nature. Biomass is a renewable energy source.

Moving and Changing

Energy cannot be created or destroyed. The same amount of energy exists today that has been around for billions of years. Energy can be transferred, or moved, from one thing to another. For example, the energy in plants is transferred to animals that eat them. Energy can also be converted, or changed, from one form to another. Burning wood converts the chemical energy stored in wood to thermal, or heat energy. It is not possible to convert all of the energy from one form to another. Some energy always changes into a form that is not useful at the time. For example, lighting a campfire during the day to cook food produces heat as well as light. The light is not needed during the day. The goal in converting energy is efficiency, or changing as much of it as possible into a usable form.

Electricity

Power is the rate at which energy is used up doing work. Usually, people refer to "power" when describing electricity. Electric power is measured in watts, which describe the rate at which an appliance uses electricity. The higher its wattage, the more electricity it uses. Below are some common household appliances and the power they use:

INCANDESCENT LIGHT BULB 60 watts

HAIR DRYER 1,250 watts

COMPUTER 360 watts

REFRIGERATOR 500 watts

Conservation Tip

Energy conservation means limiting the amount of power that we use. You can find tips on how to conserve energy, and facts about energy conservation in boxes like these.

5

Energy Problems

Fossil fuels are the most commonly used energy source in the world today. Burning fossil fuels for energy is harmful to the environment and to people's health. There have been many conflicts between countries over oil, which will likely increase as fossil fuels become more scarce. As a result of these problems, people are becoming more interested in alternative energy sources, such as biomass.

The Environment

When fossil fuels are burned for energy, greenhouse gases, such as carbon dioxide, are released into the air. Greenhouse gases trap the Sun's heat in the **atmosphere**. Scientists believe this is causing global warming, or the gradual warming of the Earth. Many scientists believe that if global warming continues, polar ice caps will melt, and global weather patterns will change, causing floods, **droughts**, and crop failures. Acid rain is another way burning fossil fuels is harming the environment. Acid rain is created when raindrops absorb a **toxic** gas, called sulfur dioxide, in the air before falling. Sulfur dioxide damages buildings and forests, and kills wildlife.

Acid rain can kill wildlife and plants.

Running on Empty

There is a limited amount of oil, coal, and natural gas in the world. Many scientists believe we may have about 100 years' worth of oil and natural gas, and 250 years' worth of coal left. As the world runs out of fossil fuels, they will become more expensive to use. Most of the technology used every day is powered by fossil fuels. Vehicles use gasoline, furnaces use coal, oil, or natural gas, and most power plants run on fossil fuels to produce electricity. To keep technology running, people will need to switch to new energy sources.

Energy Independence

Fossil fuels are found only in certain areas of the world. Many countries import, or buy in, oil from countries in the Middle East, where most of the world's supply of oil is found. If the cost to purchase oil increases, the cost to use the oil also rises. This means that driving vehicles, producing electricity, and heating buildings will be very expensive. If countries will not sell their oil, power shortages will result. To ensure a steady supply of energy that people can afford, countries need to use more sources that they already have.

Nuclear power plants run on a material called uranium. The supply of uranium, like fossil fuels, is limited. Nuclear plants do not pollute the air, but they do produce toxic waste that must be stored safely for thousands of years.

Plant Power

Plants capture and store energy from the Sun to use for food. The amount of energy that plants store each year is enough to supply the entire world with all the energy it needs!

(below) Plants make their own food by storing solar energy during a process called photosynthesis. This stored energy is passed along the food chain when people and animals eat the plants.

Storing the Sun's Energy

Plants create a type of sugar for food during a process called photosynthesis. During photosynthesis, plants convert sunlight, water, and carbon dioxide into sugar. Plants use some of the sugar immediately for food to grow and to make new plants. They store any extra energy in their roots, seeds, fruits, and stems. When animals eat plants, they receive some of this stored energy. They cannot digest every part of the plants they eat, so bits of plant material, which still has energy, end up in animal manure, or waste.

Photosynthesis

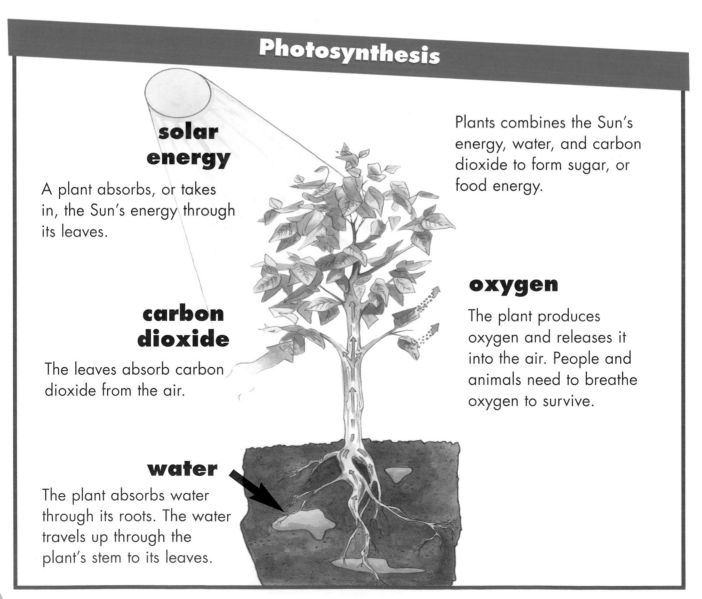

solar energy

A plant absorbs, or takes in, the Sun's energy through its leaves.

carbon dioxide

The leaves absorb carbon dioxide from the air.

water

The plant absorbs water through its roots. The water travels up through the plant's stem to its leaves.

Plants combines the Sun's energy, water, and carbon dioxide to form sugar, or food energy.

oxygen

The plant produces oxygen and releases it into the air. People and animals need to breathe oxygen to survive.

The Carbon Cycle

Burning biomass releases the carbon dioxide recently absorbed by plants back into the atmosphere. Unlike when fossil fuels are burned, this does not add to global warming because no new carbon dioxide is added to the atmosphere. The same amount of carbon dioxide the plants absorbed is released. This cycle of absorbing and releasing carbon dioxide is called the carbon cycle.

Many people believe that plants that have been modified by scientists might be dangerous, especially if they fed to livestock such as cattle. They argue that feeding these plants to animals that are then eaten by people could have health risks we do not yet know about.

Bioenergy Sources

Several types of biomass make good energy sources, including food crops such as sugar cane, sugar beets, wheat, and corn. Some biomass is what we would normally consider waste, including leftover wood, sawdust, animal manure, food scraps, lawn clippings, and the leaves and stalks left behind after harvesting plants. Plants that are grown just for bioenergy are called energy crops. The best energy crops grow quickly and regrow after harvesting. These plants include soybeans, switchgrass, bamboo, and trees such as black walnut, poplar, and willow. Scientists are working on modifying, or changing, the **genes** of some types of plants to make them grow faster and bigger, store more energy, and resist diseases, pests, and droughts.

Fueling Fires

Burning biomass is the easiest way to release its energy. Burning converts the chemical energy in biomass to heat. People in many parts of the world burn wood and other types of biomass for warmth, light, and to cook food. In the United States, Canada, Japan, Finland, and Sweden, biomass is also burned in power plants to produce electricity. Electricity that is produced using biomass is called biopower.

Two girls carry dried cow dung patties in India, where animal waste is burned for fuel.

Burning Biomass

Combustion, or burning, has been the most common way to use biomass for millions of years. Although it is the easiest way of releasing the energy in biomass, it is also the least efficient because most of the heat escapes without being used. New technology has made burning biomass more efficient by trapping and using more of the heat. The technology includes high-efficiency wood stoves and fireplaces for use in homes, and special **boilers** for use in factories.

Producing Electricity

Most power plants produce electricity by burning coal in boilers to heat water and produce steam. The steam pushes against a **turbine's** blades, causing them to spin. The spinning turbines drive **generators**, and electricity is produced. The electricity is sent to the power grid, which delivers it to homes, and other buildings. The electricity flows along cables, called lines, from power plants to reach customers across cities.

Biopower

Biomass is used to replace part or all of the coal that is burned to make steam in power plants. Burning only biomass is called direct-firing. Direct-fired plants often burn hard blocks of biomass called briquettes. Briquettes are made from bits of sawdust, grain husks, and nut shells that are pressed tightly together. Burning biomass with coal is called co-firing. Co-firing reduces the amount of pollution that is created because biomass replaces some of the coal that would normally be burned. When biomass is burned with coal, less nitrogen oxide and sulphur dioxide is released.

(above) Wood pellets made from sawdust and woodchips are a popular fuel for stoves. Pellets contain more energy than wood and burn hotter because they contain less moisture.

(below, left) The shells of nuts are used to make blocks of biomass called briquettes.

Conservation Tip

Ovens use and waste a lot of electricity or natural gas. Help conserve energy by using toaster ovens and microwaves, which use less energy than regular ovens do.

(above) Many people feel that burning solid waste greatly reduces the amount of garbage that ends up in landfills.

(left) Recyclable materials are burned in waste-to-energy plants.

Waste-to-Energy Plants

Some power plants burn solid waste, or garbage, to make the steam used to produce electricity. These are called waste-to-energy power plants. Garbage is sorted to remove recyclable materials, such as metal, glass, and plastic. The remaining garbage, including paper, cardboard, and food waste, is burned. Some people think burning garbage in waste-to-energy plants is a good way of dealing with the problem of too much waste. Other people argue that waste-to-energy plants cause pollution, waste energy, and compete with recycling, especially for materials such as paper. They also argue that **composting** food waste is better for the environment than burning it.

Garbage Burning Issues

Burning garbage releases dangerous chemicals such as dioxins, and harmful gases such as carbon monoxide and nitrogen oxides. After the garbage is burned, ash that contains harmful chemicals is left behind. The ash must be disposed of in landfills that accept toxic materials. In newer power plants, the garbage is burned at higher temperatures. This burns away the dangerous chemicals in the ash. The less dangerous ash can be disposed of in regular landfills, used to seal roads, and added to concrete to make it stronger.

CHPs

Power plants that produce electricity also produce a lot of heat. Most of this heat escapes into the atmosphere, and only a small amount is used to produce steam and generate electricity. Power plants can be more efficient by capturing the heat and using it to heat water or buildings. Power plants that burn biomass or other fuels for heat and to produce electricity are called combined heat and power plants, or CHPs.

CHPs at Work

Sawmills, paper mills, and other factories that produce waste often have CHPs on their properties. The CHPs burn the factory waste, such as sawdust and woodchips, to produce electricity to run the factory and heat to warm the buildings. The CHPs save the factories from having to pay money to dump the waste in landfills. Another benefit is that the factories do not have to purchase as much electricity from a utility company.

This power plant in Egypt is a CHP, or a combined heat and power plant. Only about 25 percent of the energy produced by burning biomass is turned into electricity.

Biogas

When biomass rots, or breaks down, it naturally produces a type of gas called biogas. Biogas contains methane, carbon dioxide, and hydrogen gases. Biomass can also be converted into gas by heating during a process called gasification. Biogas burns cleaner and more efficiently than solid biomass, and is used for heating, cooking, and producing electricity.

Landfill Gas

When landfills are full, the waste is buried under a thick layer of clay. The clay protects the waste from rain, which prevents the chemicals in the waste from being carried away by the water and into soil and water supplies. The clay also protects the waste from oxygen, and creates an environment for bacteria to feed on the waste and break it down. Bacteria are tiny organisms that can only be seen with a microscope. As bacteria digest the waste, they release methane gas. In the past, holes were drilled into the clay to release the methane to prevent a fire or explosion. Today, wells are dug into landfills to release the methane, which is piped to gas plants. At a gas plant, the methane is purified, or cleaned, to remove harmful chemicals. It is then burned to fuel power plants or put into natural gas pipelines, where it is sent to homes and used for heating and cooking.

A worker extracts a drill from a landfill in Richmond, Indiana, to release methane gas. The gas produced from the well will be purified and burned to power a generator to produce electricity.

Biodigesters

Devices called biodigesters are used to break down biomass and collect the gas it releases. Biodigesters are also called biogas plants. Manure and, sometimes, sewage is dumped into a container where it is mixed until it forms a **slurry**. It is then poured into the biodigester, which is a tank or pit, to rot. When the rotting is complete, what is left in the tank is used as a **fertilizer** to help crops grow. The gas that is produced is used as fuel for biogas cookers, water heaters, and lights. It is also burned to produce electricity.

Different Digesters

Biodigesters come in many shapes and styles, but they are all airtight and watertight. The two main types of biodigesters are batch and continuous. Batch digesters are the simplest to use. Waste is dumped into the batch digester in a single batch and is left to rot. When the waste has rotted, the biodigester is emptied, and a new batch is added. Waste is continually dumped into continuous digesters. Continuous digesters produce biogas without having to be stopped to be reloaded.

(above) These villagers in Tbilisi, in the country of Georgia, have a biodigester in their backyard. The biodigester is filled with cow dung to produce methane, which is used to power their homes.

(left) Many animal farms in North America and Europe run on manure. Large biodigesters produce biogas to run generators, which produce electricity for farm machinery and to heat buildings. On some farms, generators are connected to the power grid, so that farmers can sell their extra electricity to utility companies.

China's Biodigesters

Millions of people live on farms in rural China, where there are no gas pipelines to deliver natural gas and no power lines to deliver electricity. The main sources of energy are biomass, such as wood and rice husks, which are burned for cooking and heating. In the 1960s, the government informed people that the manure on their farms offered a better source of energy. Some families began to use small biodigesters to produce biogas, which they burned in biogas cookers and water heaters.

Biodigesters provided more than half of the energy families needed, and people collected less firewood, and breathed in less smoke from cooking fires. Biodigesters also offered a safe place to store manure, which contains harmful bacteria, so that it did not contaminate their drinking water. Today, the use of household biodigesters has spread from China to other Asian countries, including India, Vietnam, and Cambodia.

Families burn biogas in special biogas cookers and heaters to cook food and heat their homes. Biogas can also be burned to run portable generators, which produce enough electricity to run a water pump, lights, and small appliances in a home.

Gasification

Some biomass, such as wood and charcoal, can be converted into a gas called syngas. Syngas contains a mix of gases including hydrogen and carbon monoxide. To produce syngas, the biomass is burned slowly in a gasifier with very little oxygen. There are many different types of gasifiers, but all have a container where the biomass is burned, a vent through which air is added, and a vent through which the gas escapes. The gas is moved from the gasifier to a purifier where its harmful chemicals are removed. The syngas is then ready to be used. Syngas is burned in engines to power vehicles, and in boilers or gas turbines to produce electricity. The hydrogen in syngas can be separated and used to power fuel cells, which are devices that combine the gases hydrogen and oxygen to produce electricity. Fuel cells produce electricity without pollution.

(above) Villagers in India watch a television that is powered by a gasifier power plant.

(below) Illinois University's Coal Research Center in Carterville, Illinois, uses a large gasifier for experiments to produce pure hydrogen from coal. The research center is trying to turn coal into a cleaner burning fuel to power trucks and cars in the future.

Biofuels

More than half of all the fossil fuels people use are burned in vehicles. To reduce this use of fossil fuels, vehicles are being developed that run on biofuels. Biofuels are liquid fuels made from plants. Many biofuels can be used in place of gasoline and diesel to run current technology. There are five main types of biofuel: methanol, butanol, biodiesel, ethanol, and bio-oil.

Methanol

Methanol is also known as wood alcohol because it was first made from wood. Methanol was used as fuel in the late 1890s, and by the 1920s it was a popular fuel for lamps, stoves, and engines. Today, most methanol is made from natural gas, although it can also be made from wood, landfill gas, and coal. Thousands of cars that run on methanol are on the road today. Engines that burn methanol instead of gasoline emit less pollution into the air. The use of methanol also has its drawbacks. Methanol is toxic, and pollutes water when it leaks or spills. Methanol is also mixed with gasoline to fuel regular vehicles.

Biodiesel

Biodiesel is a fuel made from the oils of plants, including sunflowers, canola, soybeans, and rapeseed. The oil is mixed with alcohol, which removes **glycerin** from the oil, leaving behind biodiesel. Biodiesel was first made in the 1940s. Today, biodiesel is the fastest-growing alternative fuel in the United States and in many other countries.

This public transit bus in New York is powered by methanol. The continued use of methanol to power vehicles will reduce countries' dependence on imported oil. Using methanol will also reduce the amount of pollution that is emitted into the air.

Running on Biodiesel

Diesel engines are used to run cars, but are more often used to power large vehicles such as trucks, tractors, snowplows, and buses. A diesel engine can run on many fuels, including diesel, vegetable oils, and biodiesel. Biodiesel is either used as pure fuel, or blended with regular diesel fuel. Adding just a small amount of biodiesel to regular diesel reduces the amount of air pollution and greenhouse gases an engine releases. Biodiesel is available in the United States, England, France, Germany, Italy, Japan, and Russia, but only a few gas stations offer it for sale. For this reason, some people buy biodiesel and store it in containers to fuel their cars themselves.

(above) High oil prices and the drive for renewable energy has led to the development of biodiesel. Biodiesel is made from rapeseed, soya, and palm fruit, pictured here.

Now You're Cookin'

In the United States, Canada, and Europe, many people are altering their diesel engines so their vehicles can run on pure vegetable oil. Restaurants give people their used cooking oil to use as fuel. Before the oil can be used in a vehicle's engine, it must be filtered to remove any bits of food. Today, some vehicles have two separate fuel tanks, one for diesel fuel and the other for vegetable oil. The diesel engine is used to start the vehicle and warm up both fuel tanks. The vegetable oil must be heated to make it runny enough to use. Once the vegetable oil is warm, the driver flips a switch to use the vegetable oil in the other tank.

Ethanol

Ethanol is made from plants that naturally contain a lot of sugar. These plants include sugar cane, sugar beets, corn, and wheat. To make ethanol, the plants are ground up and mixed with water. The mixture is heated, and **yeast** is added, which causes the sugar in the mixture to ferment, or turn to alcohol. This alcohol is the biofuel ethanol. Ethanol can also be made from crop wastes including corn stalks and straw, forestry wastes such as wood chips, and grasses such as switchgrass. These plants undergo a longer process to produce ethanol because their sugars are inside **cellulose**. The cellulose must be broken down before the sugars can be separated and fermented. The ethanol produced from grasses and crop and forestry wastes is called cellulosic ethanol.

Ethanol fuels are available in Canada and the United States, but few filling stations sell them.

Running on Ethanol

Small amounts of ethanol have been added to gasoline since the 1970s. Ethanol makes gasoline burn more efficiently in the engine, so a vehicle can drive further on a tank of gas. It also reduces the amount of air pollution and other harmful chemicals vehicles release. By adding larger amounts of ethanol to gasoline, new types of fuels are created, such as E10, which is 10 percent ethanol and 90 percent gasoline. Most vehicles run on E10 without having to make changes to their engines. Millions of new vehicles can run on gasoline, E85, or a mix of both. E85 is a fuel that contains 85 percent ethanol. These vehicles are known as flexible-fuel vehicles (FFVs).

Conservation Tip

The exhaust emitted from vehicles powered by fossil fuels contains harmful chemicals that contribute to smog, air pollution, and global warming. Help save energy and the Earth by taking the bus, walking, or riding a bicycle.

Butanol

Butanol is a type of alcohol that is made from biomass and fossil fuels. Today, most butanol is made from fossil fuels because the process is easier and less expensive. To make butanol from biomass, bacteria are used to feed on corn, grass, leaves, or farm waste. As the bacteria feed, the biomass ferments. Only small amounts of butanol can be made from biomass, but scientists in the United States are trying to improve the process.

Using Butanol

Butanol can be mixed with gasoline or used alone to run vehicles. It contains more energy than other biofuels. In the future, the use of butanol may replace the use of fossil fuels for transportation, and for making products, such as plastics. Butanol may also be used to power fuel cells, because it contains hydrogen. When burned, butanol does not release the sulphur and nitrogen oxides that cause air pollution.

(above) Corn, which contains a lot of sugar, is used to make the biofuel ethanol.

Bio-oil

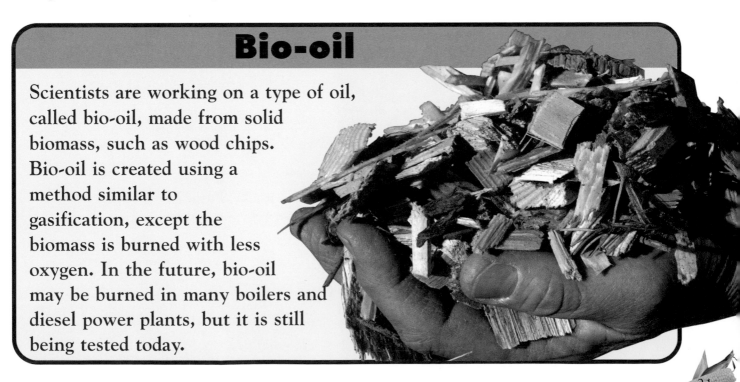

Scientists are working on a type of oil, called bio-oil, made from solid biomass, such as wood chips. Bio-oil is created using a method similar to gasification, except the biomass is burned with less oxygen. In the future, bio-oil may be burned in many boilers and diesel power plants, but it is still being tested today.

Bioenergy's History

More than a million years ago, people began burning biomass for fire and heat. Biomass has been an important source of energy ever since. It was the main energy source until the mid-1800s, when the use of coal grew. Over the past 200 years, people have developed many new ways to use biomass for energy.

Charcoal

Charcoal is one of the oldest fuels made from biomass. Charcoal is the charred remains of wood that has been burned without oxygen. As early as 3750 B.C., ancient Egyptians used charcoal as a fuel to melt copper and tin. They mixed these metals to create bronze, from which they made weapons and tools. The use of charcoal as a fuel spread throughout the Middle East, Asia, and Europe, and was used for thousands of years. By the 1800s, the wood used to make charcoal became scarce in England and other European countries. Coal began to replace charcoal because coal was easier to get, burned hotter, and was less expensive. Today, charcoal is still an important fuel in some places around the world, such as villages in Asia and Africa. Charcoal is also a popular fuel for backyard barbecues in North America.

A silversmith in Hunza, Pakistan, makes delicate silver earrings with the help of a charcoal fire.

Steam Engines

The first practical steam engine was invented in England in the early 1700s. Steam engines boil water to produce steam, which moves its parts and creates power. After years of improving upon its design, the steam engine became one of the most important innovations of the **Industrial Revolution**. Steam engines replaced water and muscle power, and were used to power machines in factories, and run steamboats and trains. Early steam engines were powered by wood or coal. As wood became scarce in Europe throughout the 1700s, coal was used more often. Coal also began to replace wood in the United States and Canada. By the mid-1800s, coal had replaced wood entirely as the fuel to power steam engines.

Gasifiers

Gasifiers have been used for heating and producing power since the mid-1800s. They became especially popular in Europe during **World War II**. During the war, gasoline was scarce because it was needed by the armed forces to fuel war vehicles, such as airplanes and tanks. People used gasifiers to run their vehicles, as well as generators to produce electricity. In the 1940s, more than one million gasifiers were used around the world. Their popularity dropped after the war, when gasoline became available again.

During World War II, oil and gasoline became very scarce in Europe. Europeans changed more than 100,000 cars and trucks to run on wood gasifiers instead of gasoline.

The Early Days

Biofuels may seem like a modern invention, but they are more than 150 years old! In the 1800s, ethanol was a popular lighting fuel for lamps. Many inventors experimented with ethanol when they began developing engines, because it was an inexpensive and easy-to-get fuel. In 1826, an American inventor named Samuel Morey received a **patent** for an engine he built that ran on ethanol and **turpentine**. Ethanol's popularity in the United States ended in 1862 when the government added a **tax** to it. Ethanol became four times more expensive than kerosene, a fuel made from oil that was used for lighting. People began buying kerosene, and ethanol was no longer used until 1906, when the government removed its tax.

"Fuel of the Future"

In the early 1900s, inventors began experimenting to find the best fuel for a new invention—the car. Many inventors believed ethanol was a better fuel than gasoline, and called it "the fuel of the future." They supported the use of ethanol because it was cleaner and safer than gasoline. Ethanol became a popular fuel in many European countries that did not have their own supply of oil to produce gasoline. In the United States, gasoline was less expensive than ethanol because the country had its own supply of oil. American oil companies also discouraged the use of alcohol fuels. Ethanol was used during World War II when gasoline was scarce, but fell out of use once gasoline became available again.

(below) German inventor Rudolph Diesel built the first diesel engine in 1890. He displayed his engine to the public in 1900, at the World Fair in Paris, France. He ran the engine on peanut oil, although it could run on a variety of plant oils.

(above) In 1908, Henry Ford designed the Model T to run on either gasoline or ethanol.

24

The Oil Crisis

After World War II, large amounts of oil were found in the Middle East. Countries around the world began buying oil from Middle Eastern countries because it was inexpensive and plentiful. In 1973, some of the countries in the Middle East refused to sell oil to the United States and European countries. Prices for oil soared because the **demand** for oil was greater than the amount that was available. Europeans and North Americans faced an energy crisis, and they became interested in alternative fuels. Ethanol became popular again, as well as fuels such as gasohol, which is known as E10 today. Governments around the world paid for research to find easier and less expensive ways to make ethanol. After the oil crisis ended in 1974, this research continued. As a result, many improvements that have lowered the cost of ethanol and other bioenergies have been made over the years.

Today, almost all cars sold in Brazil have flexible-fuel engines, which run on ethanol produced from sugar cane.

Brazil's Bio-revolution

Brazil's government decided to increase the amount of fuel it made following the 1973 oil crisis. Farmers were encouraged to grow more sugar cane, to be made into ethanol. The government paid part of the costs to make and buy ethanol, and filling stations offered ethanol to customers. The taxes on cars that ran on ethanol were lowered. Ethanol became less expensive to purchase than gasoline. By the mid-1980s, almost every car in Brazil ran on ethanol. In the 1990s, the price of oil fell, and there was a shortage of sugar cane, causing the cost to make and purchase ethanol to soar. In 2002, flexible-fuel vehicles, which run on ethanol, gasoline, or a mix of the two, became available. People could fuel their vehicles with whichever fuel was cheaper.

The Drawbacks

Biomass has many benefits, but like all energy sources, it also has drawbacks. It does create some pollution, currently costs more than fossil fuels, and environmental problems can arise if energy crops are not farmed carefully.

Competing for Crops

Crops such as sugar cane, sugar beets, corn, rice, and wheat are useful for creating biomass fuels, but they have many other important uses as well. They are used for food and to make many types of products. For example, wood chips and sawdust are used to make particleboard, animal litter, and packing material. Companies that produce fuel or electricity from biomass have to compete with many other businesses to purchase biomass. The competition can increase the price of biomass, and also lead to shortages.

Too much, Too fast

To meet increased demand for biomass, some farmers use chemical fertilizers and **pesticides** to grow bigger, healthier energy crops in less time. These chemicals pollute soil and water. Some farmers also sell all the biomass from their land, including the stubble that is left after a harvest. Stubble is a plant material normally left to rot into the soil to replace nutrients the plants used while growing. Without stubble, the soil has less nutrients and plants will not grow in it without chemicals. Stripping away stubble can also lead to soil erosion, or the loss of soil. When plant roots in stubble are removed, they can no longer hold the soil in place when it rains or is windy.

Stubble is left in fields after harvesting to help replace nutrients in the soil.

Air Pollution

Burning biomass produces less pollution than burning fossil fuels does, but it releases more pollution that other alternative energy sources such as wind or solar energy. When biomass is burned, chemicals, including carbon monoxide, sulphur dioxide, and methane are released. To reduce the amount of pollution created by burning biomass, some power plants use **scrubbers** and other devices that catch pollutants before they reach the air.

Cost Competition

To attract customers, an energy source has to cost about the same amount as fossil fuels. In many countries, biofuels and biopower cost more than energy from fossil fuels. If farmers grow more energy crops and scientists develop better ways for releasing the energy in biomass, the price for bioenergy will lower. When biorefineries, or factories that make biofuels, produce more ethanol and biodiesel, the price of these fuels will also drop. Farmers will not grow more crops, and companies will not build more biorefineries unless there is demand for their products. Currently, many people do not use biodiesel or ethanol because the fuels are too expensive to purchase or difficult to find.

(above right)Energy crops, such as switchgrasses and other grasses, can help prevent soil exhaustion and erosion. They do not take a lot of nutrients from the soil or require chemical fertilizers, as some food crops do. They have long roots that remain in the ground each year, which hold the soil in place.

The Perks

Using biomass instead of fossil fuels can help people and the planet in many ways:
- Grasses and trees can grow, and animal dung can be found almost anywhere in the world
- Biomass is a renewable resource, and will never run out
- Using biomass reduces the amount of garbage that ends up in landfills
- Biomass is a reliable energy source. The chemical energy stored in biomass is released only when it is needed
- The high demand for biofuels and bioenergy provides farmers with a steady market for their crops

Making the Change

Biomass is the largest renewable energy source in the world. In North America and Europe, bioenergy is just a small part of all the energy people use. Getting people to replace fossil fuels with biomass will require planning, time, and money. Most importantly, it will require changing the way people think about energy and energy sources.

Starting Now

It is possible to start the switch to bioenergy today. People that own flexible-fuel and diesel vehicles can fill their fuel tanks with biofuels. As biofuels become more available at filling stations, more people will likely switch to using them. Many power plants that burn coal have begun co-firing with biomass. Co-firing is an inexpensive way to increase the use of biomass, since no new equipment needs to be installed.

Better Biomass

Scientists are looking for ways to make biomass less expensive to purchase and more efficient to make. Some scientists are trying to develop energy crops that will grow faster and use less energy to plant, harvest, and turn into fuel. Other scientists are working to improve the method for making ethanol so that it costs about the same to purchase as gasoline. In the future, ethanol may be used as a clean, renewable source of hydrogen, which can be used to power fuel cells.

Fuel cell vehicles do not harm the environment because they emit water vapor instead of harmful exhaust, as vehicles that run on fossil fuels do.

Bumping Up Biomass

Switching to bioenergy on a large scale requires building new infrastructure, or networks, to grow, harvest, and store biomass. New biorefineries need to be built to process biomass, or turn it into usable fuels. Once ethanol and biodiesel are produced, they can be stored, transported, and sold using the same equipment used today for gasoline and diesel. To make biopower more efficiently, new power plants that use biogas will need to be built, and equipment that combine gas and steam turbines will need to be used. The new power plants could be twice as efficient as steam power plants, and the electricity they produce will be less expensive. Today, some of these plants are used to test how well biogas produces electricity in Sweden, Italy, Brazil, and Hawaii.

Members of Greenpeace hang a banner to encourage people to use alternative energy.

CASE STUDY

Biotown, U.S.A.

In September 2005, Reynolds, Indiana, became the first town in the world to begin making the switch to bioenergy. The town is now known as "Biotown, U.S.A." The town plans to make the switch in three phases. During Phase One, townspeople will be educated about ethanol and biodiesel, and ethanol pumps made more available. In Phase Two, the town will begin to produce electricity from biogas made in biodigesters using farm waste, manure, and trash. In Phase Three, the town will focus on producing syngas. The people of Reynolds hope to prove that energy needs can be met by using biomass.

Energy Timeline

People rely mainly on fossil fuels for energy today, but this has not always been the case. For millions of years, people's energy needs were met by using bioenergy. Biomass played an important part in our history, and it will be an even more important source of energy in the future.

(above) Wheat is used to make the biofuel ethanol.

(below) Used vegetable oil from restaurants is being used to power vehicles.

1.7 million years B.C.

Prehistoric humans use fire for heat and light.

3750 B.C.

Ancient Egyptians use charcoal for melting metal.

220 B.C.

Clay stoves are used in China to enclose cooking fires indoors.

100 B.C.

An ancient Greek named Heron creates the first steam engine.

1735

The first completely enclosed European cooking stove, called the Castrol stove, appears in France.

1826

American inventor Samuel Morey develops an engine that runs on ethanol and turpentine.

1862

The U.S. government taxes alcohol, including ethanol. Ethanol becomes more expensive than other lighting fuels.

1876

German inventor Nikolaus Otto invents an engine that runs on ethanol.

1896

American carmaker Henry Ford builds an engine known as the quadricycle, which runs on pure ethanol.

1939-1945

World War II causes shortages of oil, and ethanol and wood gasifiers become popular.

1930s-1950s

Kerosene, oil, electricity, and natural gas replace wood as the most used fuel for heating and cooking.

1973

The oil crisis sparks new interest in ethanol, wood, and other types of bioenergy.

1984

The first wood-fired power plant is built in Burlington, Vermont, U.S.A.

1989-90

Gas turbine power plants are tested for the first time in Canada and the United States.

1997

North American car manufacturers introduce new flexible-fuel vehicles.

2002

More than three million flexible-fuel vehicles are in use in the United States.

2005

An international agreement called the Kyoto Protocol is signed by 163 countries. The agreement aims to reduce the amount of carbon dioxide released into the air.

(above) Biodiesel can be made from the oil in sunflowers.

(below) Indian workers prepare wood for a gasifier, which supplies about 1,200 families with power.

Glossary

atmosphere The layers of gases surrounding Earth

boiler A vessel used to make steam for heating or power

cellulose The main substance of the cell walls of plants and of wood

chemical energy A type of energy that is stored in human bodies, plants, and oil and gas

compost To fertilize with a mixture of decaying organic matter

demand The amount wanted by buyers

digestion The process in which a body breaks down food into nutrients

drought A period of little or no rain

fertilizer A substance that helps plants grow

gene Part of an animal or plant cell that determines a characteristic that will be passed on to its offspring

generator A machine that converts mechanical energy into electric energy

glycerin A preparation of glycerol, a liquid obtained from fats and oils

Industrial Revolution A period starting in the late 1700s in England, when people began moving to cities to work in factories

organism A living thing, such as a plant or animal

patent A legal document that prevents people from using inventors' ideas for a certain period of time without giving them proper recognition and payment

pesticide A chemical used to kill harmful insects

scrubber A device used to remove impurities from a gas

slurry A thin mixture of fine particles and a liquid, such as water

tax Money collected from the people by a government to pay for public services

toxic Poisonous, or something that can kill or harm

turbine A device in which mechanical power is created by making steam, air, or flowing water turn the blades or vanes of a rotating wheel

turpentine An oil from the wood or resin of certain pine trees

World War II An international conflict that was fought from 1939 to 1945

yeast A substance made up of a type of fungi that grow quickly

Index

Printed in the U.S.A.